First Phrases from Around the World

Everyday Haitian Creole

Tricia Hoffman

Little Mitchie
an imprint of Mitchell Lane

CREATING YOUNG NONFICTION READERS

Little Mitchie books spark curiosity and support early nonfiction reading for students in Grades 2-3. Designed to build vocabulary, support second language learners, and prepare readers for middle-grade content, each book includes helpful tips for parents and educators to build confidence and deepen understanding of the world.

TIPS FOR READING NONFICTION WITH BEGINNING READERS

Talk about Nonfiction

Begin by explaining that nonfiction books give us information that is true. The book will be organized around a specific topic or idea, and we may learn new facts through reading.

Look at the Parts

Most nonfiction books have helpful features. Our *Little Mitchie* titles include color photographs and graphic aids, a table of contents, a glossary, and an index. Share the purpose of these features with your reader.

Color Photos and Graphic Aids

A lot of information can be found by "reading" photos, charts, maps, and other graphic aids found within nonfiction texts. Help your reader learn more about the different ways information can be displayed.

Table of Contents

Located at the front of the book, this list shows the big ideas within the text and the page numbers where they can be found.

Index

Located at the back of the book, an index is an alphabetical list of topics and the page numbers where they can be found.

With a little help and guidance about reading nonfiction, you can feel good about introducing a young reader to the world of *Little Mitchie* nonfiction books.

Little Mitchie is an imprint of:

Mitchell Lane
PUBLISHERS

2001 SW 31st Avenue
Hallandale, FL 33009
mitchelllanepub.com

First Edition, 2027.

Author: Tricia Hoffman
Designer: Kathy Walsh
Editor: Tricia Hoffman

Library of Congress Cataloging-in-Publication Data
Title: Everyday Haitian Creole / by Tricia Hoffman

Description: Hallandale, FL :
Mitchell Lane Publishers, [2027]

Identifiers:
Library bound ISBN: 979-8-89260-909-8
Paperback ISBN: 979-8-90145-060-4
eBook ISBN: 979-8-90145-019-2

Library of Congress Control Number: 2026931243

PHOTO CREDITS: Cover and Title pg: iukhym_vova, smile3377; Doodle Art: devitaayu, FourLeafLover, wanchana, veekicl, Rizky, mhatzapa, Kebon doodle, Asyam Design, piixypeach, syoko: istock: background, rica nohara; p 4, sugianton, glenda, Kiselev Andrey Valerevich; p 5, Maya Lab; p 6, Nolte Lourens, Sergey Novikov, Anton Albert; p 7, Eric Isselee, pyrozhenka; p 9, ViDI Studio; p 10, Prostock-studio, mavo, Julia Zavlishina; p 11, arapix; p 12, PeopleImages, Chiociolla, Chase D'animulls, BongoStock; p 13, Bet_Noire, Dragon Images; p 14, GaudiLab, Inside Creative House, takasu; p 15, Drazen Zigic, fast-stock; p 16, Dennis MacDonald; p 16, Prostock-studio, oliveromg; p 17, Roman Samborskyi; p 18, Prasannapix, Boijonell Prod;, Nevada31; p 19, Rotorhead 30A Productions; p 19, Drazen Zigic; P 20, stockpexel, New Africa, Yuganov Konstantin; p 21, Anamaria Mejia, Sergil Koval, etorres, antoniodiaz, JLco Julia Amaral; p22, Prostock-studio, Lightfield Studios; p 23, New Africa

Table of Contents

This Is Me (Sa a se mwen). 4
People and Pets (Moun ak bèt kay). 6
Today (Jodi a) 8
Morning (Maten) 10
Breakfast (Dejene) 12
School (Lekòl) 14
Time to Play (Lè pou jwe) 16
Neighborhood (Katye) 18
Dinner (Dine) 20
Night (Lannwit) 22
Index 24
About Haitian Creole. 24

This Is Me

Mwen gen nèf an.

I am nine years old.

Non mwen se Mari.

My name is Marie.

Sa a se mwen

en
one

de
two

twa
three

kat
four

senk
five

sis
six

sèt
seven

uit
eight

nèf
nine

dis
ten

People and Pets

Mwen rete ak fanmi mwen.

I live with my family.

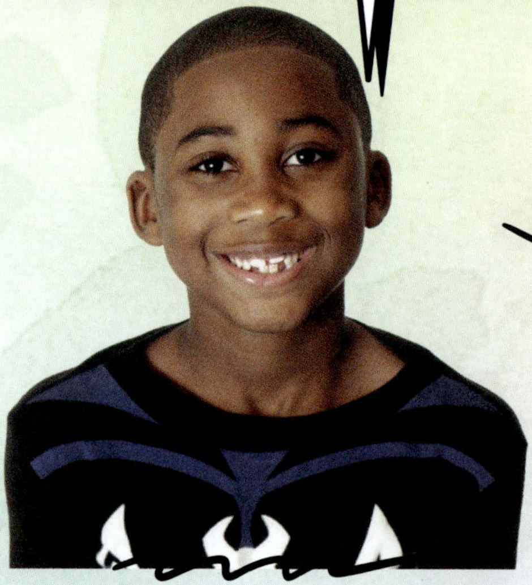

papa
father

sè
sister

manman
mother

frè
brother

Moun ak bèt kay

Mwen gen bèt kay.

I have pets.

chen
dog

chat
cat

zwazo
bird

leza
lizard

sourit
mouse

lapen
rabbit

Today

Jodi a se vandredi.

Today is Friday.

dimanch
Sunday

lendi
Monday

madi
Tuesday

mèkredi
Wednesday

jedi
Thursday

vandredi
Friday

samdi
Saturday

Mwa a se mas.

The month is March.

janvye	January
fevriye	February
mas	March
avril	April
me	May
jen	June
jiyè	July
out	August
septanm	September
oktòb	October
novanm	November
desanm	December

Jodi a

Lapli ap tonbe deyò.

It is rainy outside.

solèy
sunny

frèt
cold

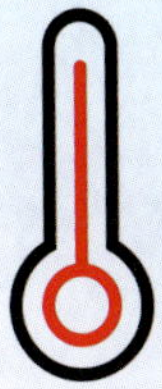

cho
hot

van
windy

Morning

Bonjou!

Good morning!

Mwen penyen cheve m.

I comb my hair.

Mwen bwose dan m.

I brush my teeth.

Maten

Mwen mete chosèt blan.

I wear white socks.

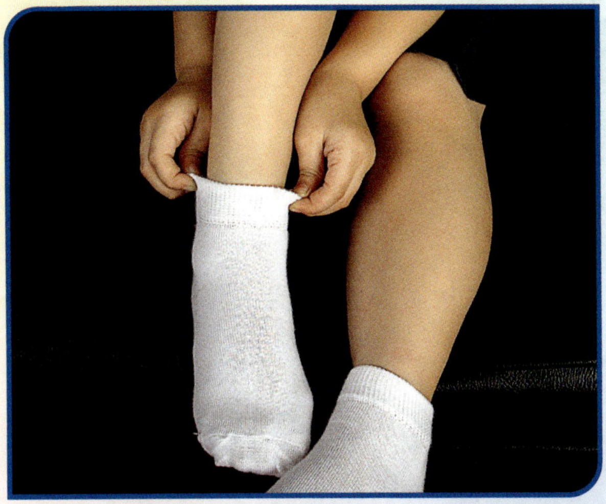

zoranj	jòn	ble	vèt	
orange	yellow	blue	green	
mov	**wouj**	**woz**	**nwa**	**blan**
purple	red	pink	black	white

Breakfast

Mwen vle sereyal pou dejene, tanpri.

I want cereal for breakfast, please.

pen griye
toast

ji zoranj
orange juice

bekonn
bacon

ze
egg

Dejene

Bis la rive.
Li lè pou ale!

The bus is here.
It is time to go!

sakado
backpack

bis lekòl
school bus

School

Mwen ale lekòl.

I go to school.

Mwen li.

I read.

Mwen fè matematik.

I do math.

Lekòl

Mwen bezwen èd.

I need help.

pwofesè

teacher

biwo

desk

Èske m ka ale nan twalèt la?

May I go to the bathroom?

Time to Play

Èske w ap jwe avè m?

Will you play with me?

Wi!

Yes!

Mwen kouri.

I run.

Mwen balanse.

I swing.

Lè pou jwe

Mwen voye yon boul.
I throw a ball.
zòrèy
ears
balon foutbòl
soccer ball
bra
arm
janm
leg
pye
foot

Neighborhood

Mwen rete nan yon katye.

I live in a neighborhood.

M fè siy ak men mwen pou zanmi mwen.

I wave to my friend.

Mwen ale nan magazen an.

I go to the store.

Katye

Konbyen sa koute?
How much does this cost?

nyaj
cloud

mòn
mountain

kay
house

motosiklèt
motorcycle

lari
street

Dinner

Èske li lè pou dine?

Is it time for dinner?

Wi, tanpri.
Yes, please.

Non, mèsi.
No, thank you.

Dine

Mwen renmen manje Ayisyen.
I like Haitian food.

bannann peze
fried plantains

griot
fried pork

pate kòde
fried pastries

Mwen renmen manje Ameriken.
I like American food.

anmbègè
hamburger

fri franse
french fries

Night

Mwen mete pijama.

I wear pajamas.

Mwen pral dòmi.

I go to bed.

Mwen fèmen je m.

I close my eyes.

Lannwit

Bòn nwi!
Good night!
pengwen
penguin
liv
book
kouvèti
blanket

Index

animals 7

body parts 17

colors 11

days of the week 8

family members 6

foods 12, 21

months of the year 8

numbers 4, 5

shopping 18, 19

weather 9

About Haitian Creole

Haitian Creole is spoken by nearly 12 million people, mostly in Haiti. It became an official language of Haiti in 1987. Haitian Creole is considered a French-based language, but it is a unique language all on its own. About 90 percent of Haitian Creole words are influenced by French. The remaining 10 percent of words are influenced by African languages, Spanish, and English. In Haitian Creole, words are pronounced as they are spelled. Haitian Creole's grammar is straightforward, so it is often described as easy to learn.